Whispers Of The Soul

Pradeep Rajput

BookLeaf
Publishing

India | USA | UK

Made with ❤ on the BookLeaf Publishing Platform
www.bookleafpub.in
www.bookleafpub.com

Dedication

To the dreamers who dare to hope,
To the hearts that have loved and lost,
To the souls searching for meaning in silence,
This book is for you.
For the ones who have wandered through the corridors
of their minds, searching for answers in echoes of the
past. For those who have stood in the storm, feeling the
weight of their own unspoken words pressing against
their chests. For the quiet fighters, the gentle souls, the
ones who carry invisible scars yet continue to move
forward—this is for you.
To the lovers who gave their hearts freely, even when
they weren't sure they would be held in return. To the
ones who have lost themselves in the beauty of a fleeting
moment, only to wake up longing for its warmth again.
To those who have watched the sun rise after a night of
endless thoughts, whispering their fears to the wind—
your emotions are seen, your journey is valid, and your
voice matters.
May these pages be a refuge for your heart, a mirror for
your soul, and a reminder that even in silence, you are
not alone.

With love,
Pradeep Rajput

Preface

There are emotions that words struggle to capture, silences that hold more meaning than spoken sentences, and whispers of the soul that echo in the quiet corners of our hearts. This book is a journey into those hidden spaces—a collection of unspoken truths, unfinished words, and the raw, unfiltered reflections of the human experience.

Life is a symphony of fleeting moments, some filled with joy, others with sorrow. We carry within us the weight of memories, the ache of lost conversations, and the longing for closure that never came. These pages attempt to give voice to those fragments of life we often leave behind—letters never sent, feelings never confessed, and roads never taken.

Each poem in this collection is an intimate whisper, inviting you to pause, reflect, and embrace the emotions that make us who we are. Whether you have loved and lost, struggled and endured, or simply wondered about the intricacies of the human heart, these words are for you. They are for the dreamers, the seekers, the broken, and the hopeful.

May these whispers find a home within your soul,
offering solace, understanding, and a reminder that you
are not alone in your journey. Let us embark on this
exploration of love, loss, healing, and hope together.

With gratitude and heart,

Pradeep Rajput

Acknowledgements

No book is ever created in isolation, and this collection would not have been possible without the unwavering support, love, and inspiration from so many.

First and foremost, I extend my deepest gratitude to my family, whose encouragement and belief in my words have given me the strength to continue writing. Your love is the foundation upon which my creativity thrives.

To my friends, who have been my sounding board and my greatest cheerleaders, thank you for listening to my musings, reading my drafts, and offering your invaluable insights. Your presence in my life is a blessing beyond words.

A heartfelt thank you to every reader who finds solace in these pages. This book is as much yours as it is mine. Your emotions, experiences, and stories breathe life into these words, and I am honored to share this journey with you.

To the countless poets, writers, and dreamers who have inspired me along the way, your art has been a beacon of light, reminding me that words have the power to heal, connect, and transform lives.

Lastly, to the silent moments, the unspoken emotions, and the whispers of the soul—thank you for teaching me that even in silence, there is poetry.

With profound appreciation,

Pradeep Rajput

1. The Unfinished Symphony

Love is an unfinished symphony,
a song that lingers long after it ends,
playing softly in the quiet corners
of a heart that still remembers.
You were the melody I never mastered,
a tune that slipped between my fingers,
a harmony I hummed in the dark
when no one else could hear.
We wrote our verses in whispers,
in stolen moments,
in the silent exchange of glances
that spoke more than words ever could.
But fate was a cruel composer,
pausing where we longed for crescendos,
cutting short the notes
that should have carried us home.
Yet still, the music lingers—
in the spaces between memories,
in the echoes of what could have been,

in the way my heart beats
to the rhythm of your name.

2

2. The Weight of Unspoken Words

If I had told you I loved you,
would the world have shifted beneath our feet?
Would time have paused,
holding its breath between heartbeats,
waiting for your answer?
Or would the sky have remained unchanged,
the wind still whispering its secrets,
the stars unmoved by my confession?
There are words that live within us,
unspoken yet heavy,
pressed into the spaces between our ribs,
tucked beneath our tongues,
like letters never sent.
I carry them with me,
in the hollow of my chest,
in the spaces where your voice once lived.
I wonder if you ever hear them—
in the silence of the night,
in the pause before sleep,

in the echo of footsteps
walking away.
I should have spoken.
I should have let the words take shape,
risked the sharp edges of truth,
even if it meant losing what we had.
Because now,
I live in the shadow of what was left unsaid,
haunted by the weight
of a love
that never had the chance to be real.

3. The Echo of Yesterday

Yesterday lingers like a ghost,
moving through my memories,
soft and silent,
never truly gone.
I still hear your laughter
in the empty spaces of my days,
a sound carried by the wind,
faint but never forgotten.
We were something once—
not quite love,
but something close enough
to leave an ache in its absence.
Time moves forward,
but yesterday clings to me,
woven into the fabric of who I am.
I see you in familiar places,
in the way the sun sets,
in the way the rain taps against my window,
in the way my heart hesitates
before letting go.

Some echoes never fade.
Some goodbyes are never final.
And maybe, just maybe,
yesterday is still waiting for us
somewhere
just beyond the horizon.

4. The Sun Will Rise Again

There are nights that stretch forever,
where dawn feels like a distant dream.
Nights when the weight of sorrow
is heavier than my own name,
when the world turns cold
and I forget what warmth feels like.
But I have learned something
in the darkest hours—
no matter how endless the night may seem,
the sun will always find its way back.
I have seen the storm rage,
watched the sky split open
with fury and grief,
felt the earth tremble beneath my feet.
Yet after the rain,
the world breathes again.
The air is fresh,
the ground softened,
the sky open, waiting.
Pain does not last forever.

No storm can last a lifetime.
Even when the night is at its darkest,
the sun will rise again—
bringing with it
another chance to begin.

5. A Love That Never Left

Love does not always die
when people leave.
It lingers in the empty spaces,
in the echoes of laughter,
in the warmth of a memory
that refuses to fade.
You are not here,
but love still exists in the way
I remember you—
in the pages of our story
that I cannot bring myself to close.
There are days when I feel you
in the soft hush of morning,
in the melody of a song we once shared,
in the quiet way my heart
still whispers your name.
Some love does not end.
It only changes shape,
becoming the air we breathe,
the dreams we visit,

the silent prayer
we whisper at night.
And perhaps, in some way,
you are still here—
not in the way you once were,
but in the love
that never truly left.

6. Footsteps on Water

They say memories fade with time,
that the past is nothing but a dream,
but I still hear your footsteps on water,
still feel your presence in the waves.
You walked into my life like a tide—
gentle, inevitable, pulling me in,
a force beyond reason,
a rhythm I could not resist.
We danced on the shores of tomorrow,
etching promises into the sand,
knowing well that the sea
always reclaims what is written there.
And yet, we believed.
We believed in forever,
in footprints that would outlast the tide,
in love that would never wash away.
But love, like water, is wild.
It moves where it wills,
slipping through fingers,
disappearing into the vast unknown.

I search for you in the waves,
in the hush of the ocean's breath,
but all I find is silence—
the echo of a love now lost at sea.
And so, I walk the shoreline alone,
watching the tide erase our past,
until even the footsteps on water
become nothing but a memory.

7. Letters Never Sent

There is a drawer in my heart,
filled with words I never gave you,
letters I wrote in the dead of night,
sealed with longing, never sent.
I wrote of the way your eyes
held entire galaxies within them,
of how your voice
felt like poetry against my skin.
I wrote of the way love bloomed,
wild and unafraid,
of the nights when silence spoke
more than words ever could.
And then I wrote of the endings—
of the slow unraveling of us,
of the way goodbyes
are never as sudden as they seem.
I never sent them,
because some things are meant
to remain unspoken,
some wounds meant to heal in silence.

But on some nights,
when the stars whisper your name,
I still take them out,
these letters to a love that once was.
And in the quiet,
I read them to the wind,
hoping that somehow,
somewhere,
you hear them too.

8. The Art of Falling

They never teach you how to fall—
not in love, not in life,
not in the way the heart
collapses under the weight of longing.
They tell you about soaring,
about the rush of beginnings,
about the thrill of the unknown.
But they never speak of the fall.
The way love crumbles
like a house built on sand,
how trust shatters
in the space of a single breath.
The way dreams slip
through trembling fingers,
how hope turns to dust
before it ever becomes real.
Falling is an art,
a lesson learned in breaking,
in the silence of empty rooms,
in the echoes of what once was.

But even in the fall,
there is beauty—
in the way the heart dares to beat again,
in the way we rise,
despite it all.

9. Beneath the Moonlight

There is something about moonlight—
how it turns the ordinary into magic,
how it drapes the world in silver,
hiding sorrow beneath its glow.
We stood beneath it once,
you and I,
whispering dreams into the night,
believing in things too fragile to hold.
The moon watched us,
silent and knowing,
as if it had seen
a thousand lovers before us,
each one believing they were different.
We were not different.
We loved,
we lost,
we became echoes beneath the stars.
And now, I stand alone,
beneath the same moonlight,

wondering if somewhere,
you do the same.

18

10. Fading Photographs

Time is a quiet thief.
It moves with soft, unhurried steps,
slipping between days and moments,
stealing away the faces we once knew.
I found an old photograph today—
a moment frozen in time,
a smile that still shines,
a love that still lingers in the paper's grain.
The ink is fading,
the corners curling like tired memories,
but the laughter captured in those frames
still echoes in the quiet of my heart.
I trace the outline of your face,
my fingers brushing against a past
that feels both near and far,
like a dream I wake up reaching for.
Time has taken many things,
but it has not taken this—
this still image of who we were,
this proof that we once existed

in a moment too beautiful to forget.
And though the colors fade,
and the years pull us further apart,
this photograph will always be here,
holding onto the love
that time cannot steal.

11. A Letter to My Younger Self

Dear younger me,
I know you feel lost sometimes,
like the world is too big,
too loud,
too unforgiving.
I know you lie awake at night
wondering if you are enough,
if you will ever find your place,
if the ache in your heart
will ever go away.
But I promise—
you will find your way.
You will learn that not all love stays,
but the right ones will.
You will realize that failure
is not an ending,
but a beginning in disguise.
You will outgrow places,
people,

versions of yourself
that no longer fit—
and that is okay.
There will be nights
when you feel alone,
when the world feels too heavy
for your small hands to hold.
But you are stronger than you think.
You will learn to carry yourself,
to stand tall even when you feel
like collapsing.
Someday, you will look back
and see that every heartbreak,
every late-night tear,
every doubt,
was shaping you into someone stronger,
someone kinder,
someone who knows their worth.
So hold on.
Brighter days are coming.
With love,
The You Who Made It.

12. The Silence Between Us

There was a time when words flowed between us,
effortless, like a river moving toward the sea.
Laughter softened our edges,
whispers filled the empty spaces,
and silence was never something to fear.
But now, silence has settled between us,
thick and unrelenting, stretching wider each day.
It lingers in the pauses between sentences,
in the glances that used to hold warmth
but now feel distant, unfamiliar.
I want to reach for you,
to fill the air with anything—
a word, a sigh, a memory—
but the silence weighs me down.
It is heavy, unmoving,
a quiet that is anything but peaceful.
Are we lost within it,
or are we simply waiting
for the courage to speak?
The silence hums like an old song,

one we used to know the words to,
but now only remember in fragments.
I wonder if you hear it too—
if it keeps you awake at night,
if it makes you ache the way it does me.
I want to ask if we can find our way back,
if the words still exist somewhere between us.
But I am afraid of the answer,
afraid that this silence has grown
too deep to cross.
So we sit here,
the weight of unspoken things
settling between us,
and I wonder—
is this how love disappears?
Not in anger,
not in goodbye,
but in the silence
that neither of us
dares to break.

13. Blossoms of the Heart

Love grows in unexpected ways. Sometimes, it arrives like the first light of morning, soft and gentle, filling every empty space with warmth. Other times, it comes like a storm, shaking everything you knew, making room for something new to bloom.

The heart is a garden, and love is what makes it flourish. It is not always easy. There are seasons of drought, when loneliness cracks the soil. There are times when fear and doubt take root, making it hard for anything new to grow. But even in the harshest winters, the promise of spring remains.

Love does not need to be perfect to be real. It is found in the small moments—

a hand reaching out, a voice that listens, a presence that stays when everything else feels uncertain. It is not just in grand gestures, but in the quiet consistency of someone who chooses to be there, over and over again.

The heart learns to open, even after pain. Wounds heal, though scars may remain. They do not make love impossible; they only show where strength was built.

Love teaches patience. It asks us to give without expecting, to trust without fear, to grow without holding back. And when it is true, it does not fade—it deepens, taking root in the soul, where it blossoms, again and again, in ways we never imagined.

14. The Roads We Never Took

There are roads I still dream about,
paths I never walked,
choices I left behind
like unread letters,
sealed with hesitation.
What if I had turned left instead of right?
What if I had stayed instead of leaving?
What if the love I let go
was the love I was meant to keep?
Regret lingers like morning fog,
a quiet weight pressing on my chest,
a whisper of something
I will never fully know.
But the truth is,
we can never walk every road.
Life is not a map with marked directions,
but a winding journey
where each step leads to another,
each turn shaping who we become.

I have spent too many nights
replaying old conversations,
imagining different endings,
trying to rewrite the past
with the ink of longing.
But even the roads we never took
lead us somewhere.
Even the choices we feared
shaped the lives we now live.
Because every untaken road
left room for another—
for new faces,
new lessons,
new love that might have never arrived
if I had chosen differently.
So maybe it's time to stop looking back,
to stop wondering about the "what ifs."
Maybe it's time to trust
that this path,
the one I am on,
is exactly where I was meant to be.
And maybe, just maybe,
the roads I never took
were never mine to walk in the first place.

15. How the Moon Loves the Sun

The moon has always loved the sun,
though they are destined to remain apart.
She lingers at the edges of dawn,
holding onto his final rays
before fading into the quiet embrace of morning.
She watches him rise,
glorious and golden,
too brilliant to notice her longing gaze.
She follows in his wake,
collecting the light he leaves behind,
cradling it in her arms
so she may glow for him when night falls.
The sun burns, radiant and unaware,
his fire too fierce to turn back.
Yet she orbits faithfully,
pulling the tides in silent devotion,
whispering his name to the stars
that have seen this love unfold
for an eternity.

They exist in an endless dance,
one arriving as the other fades,
always near, yet never touching.
But when the universe bends in their favor,
when fate grants them a fleeting moment—
they meet in a perfect eclipse,
a brief, stolen embrace
before they must part once more.
And still, she loves him.
Without expectation, without demand,
only the quiet ache of devotion.
For love is not always about holding close—
sometimes, it is about shining,
even when the one you love
is too far to feel your warmth.

16. Love in the Digital Age

Love today feels both closer and farther.
We are always connected, yet sometimes, we feel alone.
A message arrives, a heart emoji,
but can a screen ever replace a touch?
We meet through apps, through algorithms,
through carefully crafted profiles.
We fall for words on a screen,
for pictures that capture a moment,
but not the silence in between.
We type "I miss you" instead of saying it out loud.
We wait for a reply that takes hours,
wondering if love should feel like waiting.
We stare at screens late at night,
reading old conversations,
trying to feel something real in digital echoes.
Video calls replace warm embraces.
Voice notes replace whispered confessions.
Love letters have turned into disappearing texts,
here one moment, gone the next.
Yet somehow, love still finds its way.

A message at the right time,
a smile through a screen,
a connection beyond the pixels.
Because even in this fast world,
hearts still long for the same thing—
to be seen, to be heard,
to be loved beyond the screen.

17. Healing Is a Journey, Not a Destination

Healing is not a finish line you cross one day and never
look back.
It is not a single moment where everything suddenly
feels okay.
It is a slow, winding path with ups and downs,
progress and setbacks, light and darkness.
Some days, you will feel strong, as if the weight is finally
lifting.
Other days, the past will creep in, pulling you back into
old pain.
And that is okay. Healing does not mean forgetting.
It means learning to carry your pain differently.
There is no right way to heal.
No perfect timeline, no magic solution.
Some wounds close quickly, while others take years.
And some might never fully disappear,
but they become easier to live with.
Healing is in the small moments—
choosing to get out of bed when everything feels heavy,

allowing yourself to feel instead of pushing emotions
away,
letting go of what no longer serves you,
and accepting that not every question will have an
answer.
You are allowed to take your time.
You are allowed to break and rebuild as many times as
you need.
Healing is not about reaching a final point where you are
free from pain.
It is about finding ways to move forward,
even while carrying the scars.

18. The Weight of the Past, The Lightness of Now

The past is heavy.
It carries memories, regrets, and moments we wish we
could change.
It holds the words we never said, the mistakes we made,
and the people we lost along the way.
Sometimes, it feels impossible to let go.
We replay old conversations, wonder about different
choices,
and hold onto pain as if it defines who we are.
The past becomes a shadow,
following us even when we try to move forward.
But now—this moment—is light.
It is not tied to what was,
and it does not carry the weight of what could have
been.
Now is open, new, full of possibility.
It is the only place where change can happen,
where healing begins, where peace is found.
Letting go does not mean forgetting.

It means learning to live without being controlled by
what has already happened.
It means forgiving yourself for what you didn't know
then,
and allowing yourself to grow into someone new.
You don't have to carry everything.
You don't have to let the past decide who you are.
Right now, you have the choice to step forward,
lighter, freer, and open to what comes next.

19. Breaking from the Chain Within

The hardest chains to break are the ones we cannot see.
They are not made of metal, but of fear, doubt, and the
stories we tell ourselves.
They form when we believe we are not enough,
when we convince ourselves we are stuck,
when we let the past define our future.
These chains keep us in familiar places,
even when those places hurt us.
They whisper that change is too hard,
that freedom is too far,
that we are safer where we are,
even if we are unhappy.
But the truth is, the lock was never real.
The key has always been in our hands.
It is in the moment we choose to believe in something
better.
In the moment we realize we deserve more.
In the decision to walk away from what no longer serves
us.

Breaking free is not easy.
It takes time. It takes courage.
Some days, it will feel impossible.
But each small step forward weakens the grip of the
past.
Each act of self-love loosens the chains a little more.
You are not trapped.
You are not powerless.
You are stronger than the fear that holds you back.
And one day, you will look back and see—
the only thing keeping you in place was the belief that
you could not leave.

20. Unfinished Conversations

Some words never find their way out.
They linger in the space between what was said and
what was meant.
A goodbye that never happened,
an apology left unsaid,
a question with no answer.
We replay the moments in our minds,
rewriting them, imagining different endings.
What if we had spoken up?
What if they had stayed?
What if we had one more chance to say everything we
never did?
But life does not always give us closure.
Some conversations remain open,
some people leave before we are ready,
and some stories are left unfinished.
It is painful to carry words that were never spoken,
to wonder if things could have been different.
But maybe closure is not about getting an answer.

Maybe it is about accepting what cannot be changed
and finding peace in the silence left behind.
Not everything needs an ending to be complete.
Sometimes, we write our own closure.
We let go, even without the last word.
We move forward, even with unfinished conversations in
our hearts.

21. What We Owe to Ourselves

We spend so much of our lives meeting expectations—
fulfilling roles, chasing approval,
trying to be what the world wants us to be.
We give our time, our energy, our love,
sometimes until there is nothing left for ourselves.
But what about what we owe to ourselves?
Not in money, not in achievements,
but in kindness, in understanding, in freedom.
We owe ourselves the chance to be more than what
others expect.
We owe ourselves the space to grow, to make mistakes,
to live without the constant weight of perfection.
We owe ourselves rest.
Not just sleep, but real rest—
the kind that lets us breathe, that lets us exist
without feeling guilty for doing nothing.
We were not made to run on exhaustion.
We owe ourselves forgiveness.
For the choices we regret, the paths we didn't take,

the times we didn't know better.
We are still learning, still changing,
and we deserve the same grace we give to others.
We owe ourselves joy.
Not just in grand moments,
but in the small things—the quiet mornings,
the songs we love, the laughter that comes from deep
inside.
We owe ourselves the chance to feel alive,
not just to survive.
Most of all, we owe ourselves love.
Not just from others,
but from the one person who will always be with us—
ourselves.
To choose ourselves, to believe we are enough,
to live in a way that honors who we truly are.

22. The Alchemy of Love

Love is not something we stumble upon,
nor something waiting on a distant shore.
It is not a treasure to be hunted,
nor a mystery meant to be solved.
Love is crafted, shaped, and refined,
like gold tested by fire,
like rivers carving through stone,
like time whispering wisdom to those who listen.
We spend our lives searching,
chasing after fleeting illusions,
believing love is something to find.
But love is not a destination;
it is a journey into the depths of our souls.
The world teaches us to seek love in others,
to chase it through grand gestures,
to believe it comes from something outside ourselves.
But love is first an awakening within.
Only when we understand our own hearts,
only when we have embraced our own flaws,
only when we have learned to stand alone,

do we finally see love for what it is—
a light that grows, not in another,
but in the reflection of ourselves.
And when two souls, already whole,
find one another along the way,
it is not need that binds them,
but the beauty of love freely given,
love that does not demand,
love that simply is.

23. The Power Within

We move through life with our hands full,
gripping the weight of yesterday,
reaching for the uncertainty of tomorrow.
We forget that life is not waiting for us elsewhere.
It is here, now, in this breath, in this heartbeat.
Regret pulls us into the past,
trapping us in what-ifs and should-haves.
Fear drags us into the future,
building mountains out of things unseen.
And in between, life quietly passes.
But what if we let go?
What if we stopped running?
What if we stood still and listened?
The wind does not dwell on yesterday's storms.
The river does not question where it flows.
Everything that matters exists in this moment.
Love is felt in the touch of now.
Joy is found in the laughter of now.
Peace is not in what was or what will be,
but in surrendering to what is.

Close your eyes.

Feel the breath that fills your lungs.

Feel the world turning beneath your feet.

The past is a story already told.

The future is a page unwritten.

Now is the only place where life truly exists.

24. Becoming Me

I am not who I was yesterday,
and tomorrow, I will not be the same.
I am not meant to stay still,
not meant to fit into a single frame.
The world may try to define me,
to place me in a mold that does not fit.
It may tell me who to be,
how to speak, how to move, how to dream.
But I was never meant to be small.
I am a story still being written,
a canvas that is never complete.
Each mistake, a brushstroke of wisdom.
Each failure, a chapter of strength.
The road to becoming is never straight.
It twists, it turns, it breaks,
but it never stops moving.
And neither do I.
I am not searching for a final version of myself.
I am not meant to be finished.
I am meant to keep growing,

to keep evolving,
to keep becoming.

48

25. Love in a Whisper

Love does not always arrive loudly.
It does not always announce itself.
Sometimes, it lingers in the quiet,
in the spaces between words,
in the gentle way two souls recognize each other.
Love is not always grand gestures.
It is not always poetry or roses.
It is found in stolen glances,
in the comfort of silence shared,
in the quiet knowing of another's heart.
Sometimes, love is pride standing in the way.
Sometimes, it is hesitation, fear, doubt.
And yet, love endures.
It waits, it grows, it softens,
until two hearts finally see what was always there.
Love does not demand to be heard.
It does not rush or push.
It waits in the shadows,
in the unspoken words,
in the quiet promise of forever.

26. Lessons of Life

Life is not measured in years,
nor in wealth, nor in success.
It is measured in the love we give,
in the kindness we share,
in the moments that truly matter.
We chase things that fade—
money, titles, applause—
forgetting that in the end,
it is the simple things we will miss.
The sound of laughter at sunset.
The warmth of a hand in ours.
The stories passed down in whispers.
The love that lingers long after we are gone.
We believe we have time.
We push love aside for later.
We say, "One day, I'll call."
"One day, I'll forgive."
But the days slip by unnoticed.
Sit with those you love now.
Listen with your whole heart.

Let go of anger,
forgive without waiting,
speak the words you hold inside.
Life is not in the rush,
not in the chase for more.
It is in the quiet mornings,
the heartfelt goodbyes,
the hands held in joy and grief.
Do not wait for life to teach you this.
Do not wait until time has run short.
Love now. Give now.
Live now, while you still can.

27. Boundless Spirit

They told me who to be,
shaped me like clay in their hands,
molded me into something smaller,
easier to understand,
easier to control.
They taught me to silence my voice,
to shrink my dreams,
to walk the path they paved for me,
even when it led away from my soul.
For years, I followed,
believing their way was the only way,
that obedience was love,
that silence was safety,
that wildness was something to tame.
But my spirit was never meant to be caged.
Beneath the surface, it burned,
a flicker in the dark,
a whisper that grew louder—
until I could no longer ignore it.
Freedom is not in pleasing others.

It is not in seeking approval.
It is in unlearning the lies,
breaking the chains,
choosing the fire inside.
So now, I rise.
I walk with unshaken steps.
I embrace the untamed within me.
No longer afraid,
no longer asking for permission—
only living, fully, freely, finally.

28. The Echo of You

You are gone,
but you are everywhere.
In the whisper of the wind,
in the rustle of autumn leaves,
in the spaces you left behind.
Grief does not fade.
It changes shape,
softens at the edges,
but never truly leaves.
It becomes part of me,
woven into my breath,
threaded through my days.
Some days, I reach for you,
forgetting for a moment
that you are not here.
Other days, I sit in silence,
letting memories speak instead.
You live in the words you once said,
in the love you left behind.
You are the empty seat at the table,

the song that makes me pause,
the laughter I still hear in my dreams.
Love does not end with goodbye.
It lingers in the unseen,
in the echoes of all that once was,
in the spaces where you will always remain.

29. Rising Strong

Falling does not mean I have failed.
It means I tried,
I risked,
I dared to care.
The world tells me to be unshaken,
to hide my wounds,
to wear armor thick enough
to keep the pain away.
But strength is not in pretending.
It is in the breaking,
in the raw, aching truth,
in the courage to rise again.
Every scar is a lesson.
Every heartbreak is proof
that I have lived,
that I have loved,
that I have faced the storm
and chosen to keep going.
Vulnerability is not weakness.
It is the bravest thing we can be.

To stand in our truth,
to own our pain,
to rise even when the world says,
"Stay down."
So I stand again,
not untouched by struggle,
but shaped by it.
Not afraid to fall,
but unafraid to rise.

30. When Love Returns

Not all love stays forever.
Some love comes like the tide—
fierce, relentless, unstoppable—
only to retreat back to the sea.
We hold on,
thinking love is meant to last,
meant to be unshaken.
But love is a traveler,
moving through time,
changing as we change.
When love leaves,
it does not disappear.
It lingers in the songs we shared,
in the laughter that once filled the air,
in the quiet places where we once stood.
We grieve for the love that left,
aching for what once was.
But love does not vanish.
It transforms,
takes a different shape,

teaches us,
remains within us.
And sometimes,
when the time is right,
love returns.
Not always as before,
but in a new way—
softer, wiser, deeper.
Not all love stays.
But the love that matters
never truly leaves.

31. The Little Things

We carry too much,
burdened by things that will not matter.
We chase perfection,
worry about the opinions of strangers,
forgetting that joy is in the small things.
Happiness is not in flawless plans.
It is in the messy, unpolished,
ordinary moments we often overlook.
It is in the way sunlight warms our skin,
in the sound of laughter on a quiet morning,
in the freedom of knowing we do not need to be perfect
to be worthy of love.
Let go of the things that steal your peace.
Release the weight of unnecessary worries.
Say no when your heart tells you to.
Say yes when your soul craves something more.
Life is not meant to be spent
pleasing everyone,
chasing things we do not need.
In the end,

it is the little things that stay with us.
The love we shared,
the moments we allowed ourselves to truly live,
the small joys we once thought were nothing
but were, in truth, everything.

32. Unbecoming Everything I Was Told to Be

I spent years
trying to fit into a mold
that was never made for me.
They told me who to be—
soft, quiet, obedient.
Told me what to want,
what to chase,
what to fear.
I tried to be what they needed.
Tried to shrink myself
into something easier to love.
Tried to silence my own voice
so I wouldn't be too much,
too loud,
too different.
But I was never meant
to live inside their lines.
So I am unbecoming.
Unlearning the lies I was fed.

Breaking the rules
that were never mine to follow.
Reclaiming the parts of me
that I buried
to make others comfortable.
I am no longer apologizing
for taking up space.
No longer hiding
the fire in my soul.
No longer asking
for permission to exist
as I am.
This is my becoming.
Not into something new,
but into the person
I was always meant to be.

33. Somewhere in Another Life

Somewhere in another life,
we did not let go.
We found a way,
met in the middle,
chose each other in the end.
I see glimpses of that life
in dreams I cannot hold onto,
in the spaces between my thoughts,
in the ache that never fully fades.
Somewhere, in a world
that does not exist,
we are still us—
unbroken, untouched by time,
free from the mistakes
that pulled us apart.
Maybe in that life,
we were ready for love.
Maybe in that life,
timing was on our side.

Maybe in that life,
we did not have to say goodbye.
But this is not that life.
And no matter how much I ache for it,
this is the only life we have.
One where we loved,
where we lost,
where we became strangers
to the people we used to be.
Still,
on certain nights,
I like to believe
that somewhere,
we made it.

34. Even the Broken Can Still Shine

They told me broken things lose their worth,
that scars make you less,
that cracks mean you are no longer whole.
But I have learned
that broken does not mean ruined.
That even shattered pieces
can catch the light.
I have seen stars shine in the darkest sky,
have watched flowers bloom
in the cracks of forgotten streets,
have felt love grow
in places I thought were too damaged to hold it.
Even the broken can still shine.
Not despite their pain,
but because of it.
Every scar tells a story.
Every fracture is proof
that we survived.
So do not turn away from your wounds.

Let them breathe,
let them be seen.
You are not unworthy.
You are not less.
You are living proof
that light can find its way
through even the deepest cracks.

35. What the Moon Knows About Me

The moon has seen me
in my quietest hours,
when the world is asleep
and only my thoughts remain.
It knows the weight I carry,
the dreams I whisper into the dark,
the regrets that press against my ribs
like unsaid prayers.
The moon has watched me
stand at the edge of my sorrow,
wondering if I will ever be enough,
if the past will always own me,
if healing is more than just an illusion.
And yet,
night after night,
the moon rises,
soft, unwavering,
as if to remind me—
even in darkness,

there is light.
It does not ask me to be whole.
It does not demand my pain to disappear.
It simply exists,
as I do,
a quiet companion in the vastness of the night.
The moon knows my fears,
my loneliness,
my unspoken hopes.
And still, it stays.
Perhaps,
that is enough.

36. If Only Time Had Waited

Time does not ask,
does not pause,
does not wait for us to catch our breath.
It moves forward,
pulling us along
whether we are ready or not.
I wonder,
if time had waited,
would we have found a different ending?
Would I have learned to love myself sooner?
Would I have said the words
I never found the courage to speak?
Would I have held on longer,
or let go faster?
There were moments I needed more time—
seconds that slipped through my fingers,
conversations cut short,
goodbyes that came too soon.
But time did not wait.

And maybe it was never meant to.
Maybe life is not about
getting more time,
but making the most of the time we have.
Still,
on quiet nights,
I can't help but wonder
what could have been
if only time had waited.

37. What If We Had Stayed?

There are nights
when your name still lingers
on the edge of my lips,
when I close my eyes
and see the life
we never lived.
I wonder—
what if we had stayed?
Would we have learned
to love each other better?
To fight a little less,
to listen a little more?
Would we have found a way
to meet in the middle,
Instead of watching the distance grow?
Or were we always meant
to be a lesson,
not a forever?
Some love stories
are not written to last.

Some are just passing storms—
beautiful,
wild,
meant to shake us,
but never to stay.
And yet,
on quiet nights,
I still wonder
if maybe,
in another life,
we found a way.
What if we had stayed?
Would we have been happy?
Or would we still have lost ourselves
trying to hold on?
I will never know.
But still,
I wonder.

38. Soft Hearts Still Rise

They told me that softness
was a weakness,
that to survive in this world,
I had to be steel,
had to harden,
had to learn to be cold.
So, I tried.
I silenced the part of me
that loved too deeply,
that forgave too easily,
that felt everything too much.
But the world did not get easier.
The pain did not disappear.
And in my attempt to protect myself,
I lost the most beautiful parts of me.
I forgot that softness
is not the absence of strength.
It is its purest form.
It is choosing to love
when you have every reason not to.

It is showing kindness
when the world has only given you cruelty.
It is holding onto hope
even when your hands are trembling.
Soft hearts still rise.
Not because they are unbreakable,
but because they refuse to stay broken.
They rise in quiet courage,
in gentle persistence,
in the unwavering belief
that love—
no matter how much it hurts—
is still worth it.

39. The Road Back to Myself

For years, I wandered,
chasing dreams that weren't mine,
wearing masks that didn't fit,
trying to become someone
the world could love.
I lost myself in expectations,
in the weight of what I should be,
in the voices that told me
who I was
was never enough.
But something in me—
something quiet,
something steady—
refused to disappear.
One day, I woke up
and realized I had spent so long
trying to be everything for everyone
that I had forgotten
how to be myself.
So, I chose to begin again.

Not by running forward,
but by retracing my steps,
by unlearning the lies I believed,
by collecting the pieces of me
that I had left behind.
The road back to myself
was not easy.
It was slow,
filled with doubts,
haunted by the voices
that tried to pull me back.
But step by step,
I returned.
I learned to love my own voice,
to stand in my truth,
to embrace the person
I had been all along.
And now,
I am here.
Not lost.
Not broken.
Just me.
Finally, me.

40. You Are Still Here

The world has tried to break you,
but look at you—
still standing,
still breathing,
still choosing to hope.
There were nights
when the weight of the sky
felt too heavy on your shoulders.
Mornings when getting out of bed
felt like lifting mountains.
Days when your own reflection
felt like a stranger you no longer recognized.
And yet,
you are still here.
You have known pain
so deep it left cracks in your soul,
loss that stole the color from your world,
storms that shook the very ground
beneath your feet.
But through it all,

you kept moving forward,
even when every step felt impossible.
Do you see your strength?
Not in loud victories,
not in grand gestures,
but in the simple act of surviving,
of waking up
and facing another day,
of choosing to believe
that maybe, just maybe,
something good still waits for you.
You are not defined by what you have lost,
by the battles you have fought,
by the scars you carry.
You are defined by your resilience,
by the fire that refused to go out,
by the quiet whisper in your heart that said,
"Keep going."
And here you are.
Still here.
Still standing.
Still becoming.

41. Breathe, Let Go, Begin Again

You are not bound to yesterday.
You do not have to carry
the weight of old mistakes,
the echoes of lost chances,
the regret that lingers like a shadow.
Breathe.
Feel the air filling your lungs,
feel the world moving forward
with or without you.
Time does not stop for the past,
and neither should you.
Let go.
Let go of the words left unsaid,
the moments that slipped through your hands,
the dreams that never found wings.
Let go of the anger,
the sorrow,
the stories that no longer serve you.
They were part of you, yes—

but they are not you.
Begin again.
With the sunrise,
with a deep inhale,
with a quiet whisper to yourself:
"I am still here."
There is no shame in starting over,
no weakness in admitting
that you need a new chapter.
The trees shed their leaves each season,
the moon disappears and returns,
the waves retreat only to rise again.
So why should you fear
beginning anew?
You are allowed to change.
You are allowed to leave behind
what no longer feels like home.
You are allowed to rewrite your story,
to step forward
without looking back.
Breathe.
Let go.
Begin again.

42. Love, Without Asking

Love should not be earned,
not be proven,
not be begged for.
It should be given freely,
like air,
like the sun on your face.
Too often, we are taught
that love is something to work for,
that we must be worthy,
that we must be enough.
We change ourselves,
bend, shrink, shape our hearts
into something smaller,
something more acceptable,
something easier to love.
But love is not a prize
for the ones who are perfect.
It is not a locked door
with a key hidden in achievements,
beauty, or obedience.

Real love does not demand proof.
It does not measure your worth
by how much you can give,
by how much of yourself
you are willing to lose.
Love should feel like an open sky,
not a cage you fight to escape from.
Love should let you breathe,
not suffocate you.
It should lift you higher,
not weigh you down.
And if love asks for conditions,
if it makes you beg,
if it holds you hostage
to expectations, guilt, or fear—
then it is not love at all.
The love that is meant for you
will not ask you to change
who you are.
It will find you as you are,
and it will stay.

43. The Quietness of Love

Love does not arrive like thunder,
not always loud, not always storming in.
Sometimes, it is soft, like early morning light,
spreading across your skin, touching gently.
It does not need grand gestures,
no fireworks, no perfect words.
Love is found in the way you pour my tea,
knowing exactly how much sugar I take.
It is in the way you wait for me,
when I pause to tie my hair,
or when you walk beside me,
never too far, never too fast.
Love does not rush, it does not demand,
it does not ask to be noticed.
It exists in the spaces between words,
in the silence we do not need to fill.
It is in the knowing glances,
in the way your hands reach for mine,
not to pull, not to hold,
just to remind me—you are here.

The world moves, changes, fades,
but love stays in the quiet moments,
in the warmth of shared stillness,
where nothing needs to be said,
yet everything is understood.

44. The Shape of Happiness

Happiness is not a finish line,
not a destination waiting to be reached.
It is in the small moments, the unnoticed hours,
in the little things that often go unseen.
It is in the scent of wet earth after the rain,
the first sip of morning chai,
the laughter of a child playing on the street,
barefoot, free, without thought.
It is in the golden light slipping through curtains,
warming the floor, touching your face,
or in the way the wind moves through trees,
whispering secrets only nature understands.
We chase happiness as if it runs away,
as if it hides, as if it needs to be found.
But happiness is never missing,
only waiting to be noticed, to be felt.
It lingers in the spaces between breaths,
in the pause before a smile,
in the warmth of a hand resting on yours.
It is not meant to be caught,

only lived, only embraced,
only held gently before it moves again,
like a passing breeze,
like sunlight through leaves.

45. A Letter to the Weary Soul

Rest, my love, rest.
The weight you carry is heavy,
the road you walk is long,
but you do not have to rush.
The world will not leave you behind.
Time is not slipping through your fingers.
You are not late. You are not lost.
You are exactly where you need to be.
The river does not fight the stones,
the sky does not rush the sun,
they move, they change,
but they do not break themselves to fit the world.
Neither should you.
Breathe. Let go of the weight for a while.
Sit beneath the shade of an old tree,
feel the breeze on your skin,
watch the leaves move without fear of falling.
You were never meant to break,
only to bend, only to heal,

only to grow again.
The road will wait for you.
The dreams you left behind
are still yours to hold.
Rest now.
The sun will rise again,
and so will you.

46. Love in the Details

Love does not live in grand moments,
not in candlelit dinners, not in poetry,
not in words spoken too often
until they lose their meaning.
Love lives in the smallest things,
in the unspoken, in the unnoticed.
It is in the way your fingers trace circles
on the back of my hand as we talk.
In the way you remember which side of the bed
I like to sleep on,
without me ever needing to tell you.
It is in waiting when I stop to look at books,
in making my tea just right,
in sharing the last bite of dessert,
without needing to be asked.
Love is in the quiet gestures,
the ones too small to be seen,
but too deep to be ignored.
It does not need to be proven,
it only needs to be felt.

And in the smallest of moments,
it is the loudest thing of all.

91

47. The Fire Within

There is a fire inside you,
even on the days you feel only smoke,
even when the world makes you doubt
that it ever burned at all.
It does not matter if the flame is small,
if it flickers in the wind,
if it hides beneath the ashes
of all that you have lost.
Fire does not forget how to burn.
It waits. It breathes.
It gathers strength in the quiet,
in the darkness, in the silence.
The world will tell you
that you are not enough,
that your dreams are too big,
your voice too small,
your steps too slow.
Do not listen.
The sun does not ask
if it is worthy to rise.

The river does not question
if it deserves to flow.
You were meant to move,
to speak, to shine.
Not for the world, not for applause,
but because the fire in you
was never meant to go out.
Even if you cannot see it today,
even if all you feel is smoke,
know this—
the fire is still there,
waiting for you to breathe.
So inhale.
Rise.
Burn bright.

48. The Unfinished Song

Life is not a perfect melody,
not a song that flows without pause.
It is filled with missing notes,
forgotten words,
melodies that do not always fit together.
There are pauses where there should be music,
there are silences that stretch too long.
Some days, it feels like
the song was never meant to be sung.
And yet, it continues.
Even when the rhythm stumbles,
even when the melody shifts,
even when you forget the words—
the music moves forward.
You do not have to wait for perfection.
You do not have to know every note.
Sing anyway.
Sing even if your voice shakes,
even if the words falter,
even if the tune is unfamiliar.

For the song of life
was never meant to be flawless,
only meant to be lived.
Let the music carry you,
let it rise and fall,
let it change and grow.
No song is ever truly complete,
no melody is ever truly lost.
So keep singing,
even in the quietest moments,
even when no one listens.
Your song is still yours,
unfinished but beautiful.

49. The Beauty of an Ordinary Life

Not every story needs adventure,
not every life needs to be grand.
There is beauty in the small things,
in the quiet moments,
in the life lived simply, without rush.
It is in the smell of fresh rotis,
warm and soft,
waiting on a plate in the kitchen.
It is in the sound of bangles clinking
as hands move through the day.
It is in the laughter of a child,
running barefoot in the street,
without worry, without hesitation,
as if the world itself is made of joy.
We spend our days chasing something bigger,
as if happiness is hidden far away,
as if it must be earned,
as if we are running out of time.
But sometimes, joy is in the stillness—

in a cool breeze after a long summer,
in the first sip of chai at dawn,
in the way light falls on an old wooden door.
The world tells us to dream bigger,
to want more, to run faster.
But happiness is here,
in the life we already live,
in the moments we almost forget to see.
Pause. Look. Feel.
This ordinary life is already beautiful.

50. You Are Enough

You do not have to chase the world,
do not have to run faster,
do not have to prove your worth
to anyone who does not see it.
You were never meant to fit into small spaces,
never meant to shrink yourself
just to make others comfortable.
You do not need louder words,
a stronger voice,
a different face,
a new version of yourself
to be worthy of love.
You are enough—
as you are,
as you have always been.
Not because of what you have done,
not because of what you will do,
but simply because you exist,
because you breathe,
because your heart beats its own rhythm

without asking for permission.
Some may not see it,
some may not understand,
but their blindness does not make you less,
their silence does not make you small.
Stand as you are.
Take up space.
Let your voice rise,
not for the world,
but for yourself.
You do not have to be perfect,
do not have to be everything,
do not have to chase approval
to be whole.
You have always been enough,
even on the days
you do not feel it.
Even in your quietest moments,
even in your doubts—
you are already complete.